FROM:

____

TO:

____

SOMEONE THAT CAN DO ANYTHING - WHO WE CALL GOD - CREATED THIS GROUND BELOW - CALLED EARTH...

AND HEAVEN IN THE SKIES.
GOD'S POWER IS SO GREAT
THAT IT CAN'T BE MEASURED -
IT CAN'T BE QUANTIFIED.

HUMANS ARE MADE IN GOD'S IMAGE. HE MADE US ALL DIFFERENT COLORS TOO. BUT, ALL THAT STUFF IS SUPERFICIAL. WE ALL LOOK LIKE GOD. I DO AND SO DO YOU.

GOD CHOSE SOME BLESSED PEOPLE TO WRITE DOWN HIS WORDS IN A BOOK. IT'S CALLED THE BIBLE AND IT'S IMPORTANT. SO, LET'S TAKE A CLOSER LOOK!

PEOPLE REFER TO THE BIBLE BY A **MULTIPLE** WORDS. FOR EXAMPLE, SINCE WE BELIEVE IT CAME FROM STRAIGHT FROM GOD, IT'S ALSO CALLED "GOD'S WORD".

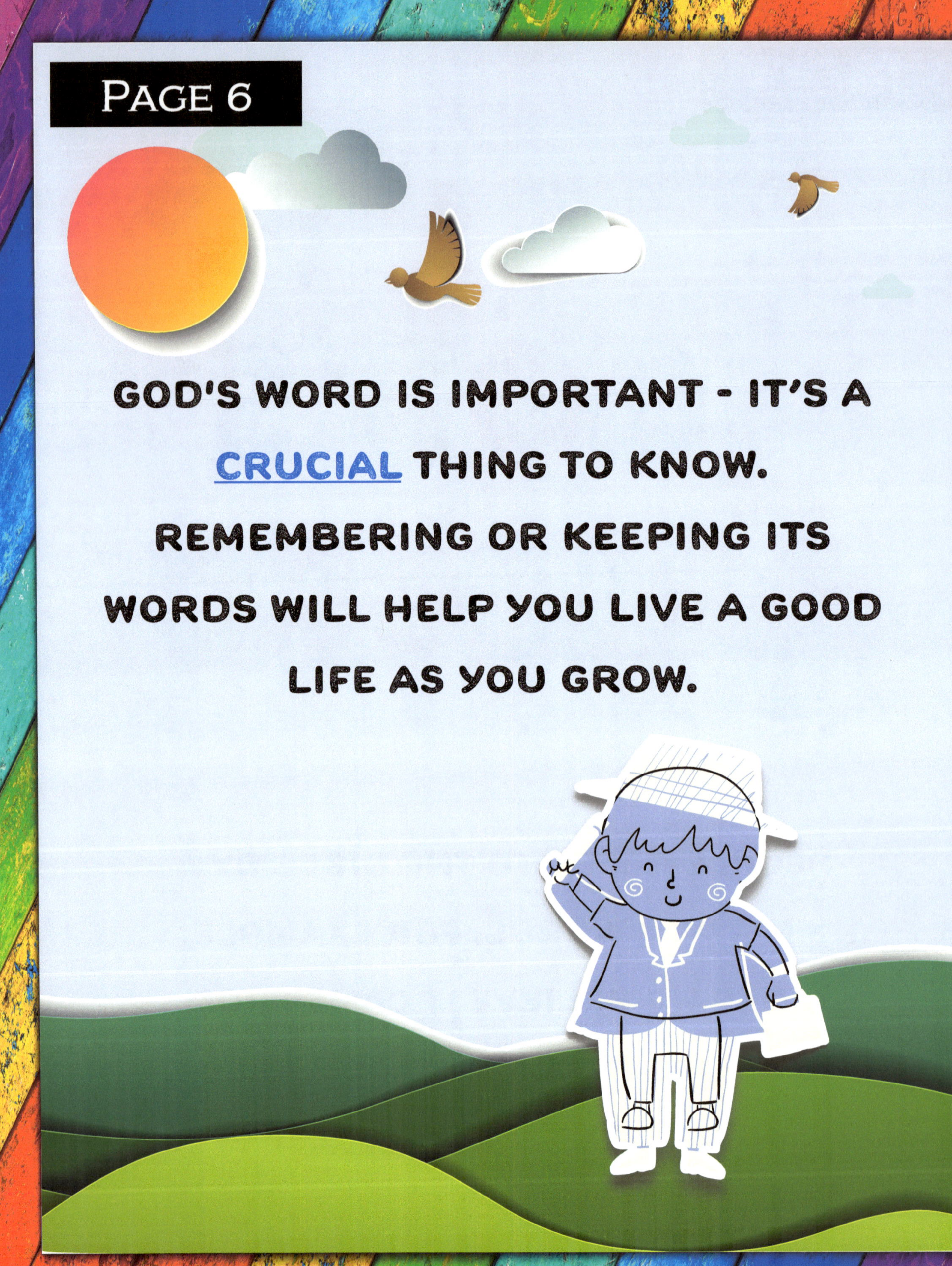

PAGE 6
GOD'S WORD IS IMPORTANT - IT'S A CRUCIAL THING TO KNOW. REMEMBERING OR KEEPING ITS WORDS WILL HELP YOU LIVE A GOOD LIFE AS YOU GROW.

REMEMBER THAT GOD LOVES US ALWAYS – THAT MEANS THROUGH THIN OR THICK.

HE EVEN SENDS ANGELS TO
WATCH OVER US LIKE WHEN
WE'RE ASLEEP OR SICK.

WE REALLY BELIEVE THE THINGS THE BIBLE TELLS US. REALLY BELIEVING SOMETHING LIKE THAT IS A SPECIAL THING CALLED TRUST.

GOD SENT HIS ONLY SON, JESUS, WHO DIED TO SAVE US FROM A BAD PLACE CALLED HELL. HE CALLED THIS THE "GOOD NEWS" AND SAID THAT WE SHOULD FIND LOTS OF PEOPLE TO TELL.

DO YOU WANT TO BE A GOOD PERSON? I DO AND SO SHOULD YOU. SO, LET'S TALK A LITTLE BIT ABOUT WHAT YOU NEED TO DO.

WHEN PEOPLE ARE HURT OR SAD, YOU SHOULD SHOW THEM THAT YOU CARE.

TAKE SOME TIME TO TALK TO GOD OR JESUS. THAT'S A SPECIAL TIME CALLED PRAYER.

JESUS SAID SINCE GOD LOVES US,

WE MUST LOVE ONE ANOTHER.

BELIEVING IN GOD MAKE US ONE BIG FAMILY. WE'RE ALL SISTERS AND BROTHERS!

SO, BEING NICE AND LOVING TO OTHERS IS THE BEST SIGN...

THAT WE'RE GOOD PEOPLE CALLED CHRISTIANS WHO TRY TO KEEP GOD FIRST IN OUR LIVES.

KNOW THAT GOD ALWAYS ANSWERS OUR PRAYERS. BUT, HE SAYS "NO" SOMETIMES.

SATAN IS THE DEVIL WHO LIVES IN HELL AND TELLS US LIES. THAT'S CALLED LYING AND IT MEANS HE SAYS THINGS THAT AREN'T TRUE. LYING IS A REALLY, REALLY BAD THING TO DO.

DOING A BAD THING IS WRONG. IT'S WHAT WE CALL A SIN. SINCE HE ENCOURAGES US TO BE BAD, WE REBUKE SATAN! THAT MEANS THAT WE TELL HIM TO LEAVE US ALONE AND GO AWAY...

BEAUSE WE BELONG TO JESUS - **THE TRUTH, THE LIFE, AND THE WAY.**

FOLLOW JESUS TO GOD

AND YOU'LL LIVE A GOOD LIFE.

YOU'LL BE DOING A-OKAY.

IF YOU DO A GOOD JOB, JESUS WILL GIVE YOU A PRIZE WHEN HE COMES BACK ON JUDGEMENT DAY.

WE'RE HAPPY TO TELL PEOPLE WHAT WE BELIEVE. THAT MEANS WE PROFESS OUR FAITH. TO DO THAT YOU JUST HAVE TO SAY,

"I LOVE GOD AND DO MY BEST
TO LISTEN AND BE KIND EVERYDAY."

JESUS SAID, GOD FORGIVES US WHEN WE SIN. SINCE JESUS DIED TO SAVE US, WE CAN NOW GO TO HEAVEN WHEN OUR LIFE ENDS.

FORGIVENESS IS SUCH A WONDERFUL THING! SO WE PRAISE GOD - THAT MEANS WE SAY GOOD THINGS ABOUT HIM, DANCE, AND SING.

"AMEN" MEANS THAT YOU BELIEVE
WHAT JESUS SAID IS TRUE.
ALWAYS REMEMBER HE SAID
TO LOVE ONE ANOTHER THE WAY
GOD WILL ALWAYS LOVE YOU.

DO YOU KNOW WHAT WE SAY WHEN OUR PRAYERS COME TO AN END? WE ALWAYS ENTHUSIASTICALLY SAY "AMEN"!

VOCABULARY

AMEN = WE BELIEVE

A-OKAY = ALL THE WAY GOOD

BLESSED - CHOSEN BY GOD

CHRISTIANS = PEOPLE TRUST AND WHO FOLLOW JESUS

CRUCIAL = SUPER IMPORTANT

ENTHUSIASTICALLY = TO BE HAPPY AND EXCITED TO SAY OR DO SOMETHING

VOCABULARY

FORGIVENESS = TO TELL SOMEONE THAT IT'S OKAY AFTER THEY'VE DONE SOMETHING BAD

GOOD NEWS = THAT JESUS SAVED US FROM HELL SO WE CAN GO TO HEAVEN - IF WE'RE GOOD - AFTER WE DIE.

HEAVEN = A GOOD PLACE IN THE SKY WHERE GOD AND THE ANGELS LIVE.

HELL = A BAD PLACE FULL OF FIRE AND BELOW THE GROUND WHERE SATAN LIVES.

HUMANS = PEOPLE

VOCABULARY

IMAGE = TO LOOK LIKE SOMETHING. THE WAY YOU LOOK LIKE YOUR PICTURE; BUT, THE PICTURE ISN'T YOU.

JUDGEMENT DAY = WHEN JESUS COMES BACK TO EARTH AND DECIDES WHO WAS GOOD AND GETS A PRIZE.

KIND = BEING NICE

LIES = SAYING SOMETHING THAT'S NOT TRUE

LYING = WHEN SOMEONE LIES OR SAYS THINGS THAT ARE NOT TRUE

VOCABULARY

REBUKE = TO TELL SOMEONE THAT THEY'RE DOING SOMETHING REALLY BAD

SIN = DOING SOMETHING BAD

THE TRUTH, LIFE, AND THE WAY = JESUS IS HOW WE DETERMINE WHAT'S RIGHT AND WRONG. JESUS IS THE WAY TO A GOOD LIFE AND HEAVEN.

THIN OR THICK = THROUGH GOOD OR BAD

TRUST = TO REALLY BELIEVE SOMETHING

EARTH

SKY =

HEAVEN

GROUND =

EARTH

POWER =
REALLY STRONG

NOT QUANTIFIED = CAN'T BE COUNTED

[LIKE YOU CAN'T COUNT ALL THE STARS IN THE SKY]

BIBLE =
GOD'S WORD

MULTIPLE =
MORE THAN ONE

HEAVEN =
ANGELS

HUMANS =
PEOPLE

SUPERFICIAL =
ONLY ON THE
OUTSIDE

CROSS

SKY = HEAVEN

HELL

PRAY OR

PRAYER

ELLIPSES [EE-LIPS-SEES] = STORY CONTINUES ON NEXT PAGE

SATAN
THE DEVIL